D1366059

GRATITUDE JOURNAL FOR KIDS

THIS BOOK BELONGS TO

_____

_____

_____

_____

_____

TODAY I AM GRATEFUL FOR...

DATE: _____

_____
_____
_____
_____
_____
_____
_____

SOMETHING AWESOME THAT HAPPENED TODAY

_____
_____
_____
_____
_____
_____
_____
_____
_____

MY LEVEL OF HAPPINESS

TODAY I AM GRATEFUL FOR...

DATE: _____

_____

_____

_____

_____

_____

_____

_____

SOMETHING AWESOME THAT HAPPENED TODAY

_____

_____

_____

_____

_____

_____

_____

_____

MY LEVEL OF HAPPINESS

TODAY I AM GRATEFUL FOR...

DATE: _____

_____

_____

_____

_____

_____

_____

_____

SOMETHING AWESOME THAT HAPPENED TODAY

_____

_____

_____

_____

_____

_____

_____

_____

_____

MY LEVEL OF HAPPINESS

TODAY I AM GRATEFUL FOR...

DATE: _____

_____

_____

_____

_____

_____

_____

_____

SOMETHING AWESOME THAT HAPPENED TODAY

_____

_____

_____

_____

_____

_____

_____

_____

_____

MY LEVEL OF HAPPINESS

TODAY I AM GRATEFUL FOR...

DATE: _____

_____
_____
_____
_____
_____
_____
_____

SOMETHING AWESOME THAT HAPPENED TODAY

_____
_____
_____
_____
_____
_____
_____
_____
_____
_____

MY LEVEL OF HAPPINESS

TODAY I AM GRATEFUL FOR...

DATE: _____

_____
_____
_____
_____
_____
_____
_____
_____
_____

SOMETHING AWESOME THAT HAPPENED TODAY

_____
_____
_____
_____
_____
_____
_____
_____
_____
_____
_____

MY LEVEL OF HAPPINESS

TODAY I AM GRATEFUL FOR...

DATE: _____

_____
_____
_____
_____
_____
_____
_____
_____

SOMETHING AWESOME THAT HAPPENED TODAY

_____
_____
_____
_____
_____
_____
_____
_____
_____
_____

MY LEVEL OF HAPPINESS

TODAY I AM GRATEFUL FOR...

DATE: _____

_____
_____
_____
_____
_____
_____
_____

SOMETHING AWESOME THAT HAPPENED TODAY

_____
_____
_____
_____
_____
_____
_____
_____

MY LEVEL OF HAPPINESS

TODAY I AM GRATEFUL FOR...

DATE:

_____
_____
_____
_____
_____
_____
_____

SOMETHING AWESOME THAT HAPPENED TODAY

_____
_____
_____
_____
_____
_____
_____
_____
_____
_____

MY LEVEL OF HAPPINESS

TODAY I AM GRATEFUL FOR...

DATE: _____

_____

_____

_____

_____

_____

_____

_____

SOMETHING AWESOME THAT HAPPENED TODAY

_____

_____

_____

_____

_____

_____

_____

_____

_____

MY LEVEL OF HAPPINESS

TODAY I AM GRATEFUL FOR...

DATE: _____

_____
_____
_____
_____
_____
_____
_____
_____

SOMETHING AWESOME THAT HAPPENED TODAY

_____
_____
_____
_____
_____
_____
_____
_____
_____
_____

MY LEVEL OF HAPPINESS

TODAY I AM GRATEFUL FOR...

DATE: _____

_____
_____
_____
_____
_____
_____
_____

SOMETHING AWESOME THAT HAPPENED TODAY

_____
_____
_____
_____
_____
_____
_____
_____

MY LEVEL OF HAPPINESS

TODAY I AM GRATEFUL FOR...

DATE: _____

_____

_____

_____

_____

_____

_____

_____

SOMETHING AWESOME THAT HAPPENED TODAY

_____

_____

_____

_____

_____

_____

_____

_____

_____

MY LEVEL OF HAPPINESS

TODAY I AM GRATEFUL FOR...

DATE: _____

_____

_____

_____

_____

_____

_____

_____

SOMETHING AWESOME THAT HAPPENED TODAY

_____

_____

_____

_____

_____

_____

_____

_____

_____

_____

MY LEVEL OF HAPPINESS

TODAY I AM GRATEFUL FOR...

DATE: _____

_____
_____
_____
_____
_____
_____
_____
_____

SOMETHING AWESOME THAT HAPPENED TODAY

_____
_____
_____
_____
_____
_____
_____
_____
_____
_____
_____

MY LEVEL OF HAPPINESS

TODAY I AM GRATEFUL FOR...

DATE: _____

_____
_____
_____
_____
_____
_____
_____

SOMETHING AWESOME THAT HAPPENED TODAY

_____
_____
_____
_____
_____
_____
_____
_____
_____

MY LEVEL OF HAPPINESS

TODAY I AM GRATEFUL FOR...

DATE: _____

_____
_____
_____
_____
_____
_____
_____

SOMETHING AWESOME THAT HAPPENED TODAY

_____
_____
_____
_____
_____
_____
_____
_____
_____
_____
_____

MY LEVEL OF HAPPINESS

TODAY I AM GRATEFUL FOR...

DATE: _____

_____

_____

_____

_____

_____

_____

_____

SOMETHING AWESOME THAT HAPPENED TODAY

MY LEVEL OF HAPPINESS

TODAY I AM GRATEFUL FOR...   DATE: _____

_____

_____

_____

_____

_____

_____

_____

_____

SOMETHING AWESOME THAT HAPPENED TODAY

MY LEVEL OF HAPPINESS

TODAY I AM GRATEFUL FOR...   DATE: _____

_____

_____

_____

_____

_____

_____

_____

_____

SOMETHING AWESOME THAT HAPPENED TODAY

MY LEVEL OF HAPPINESS

TODAY I AM GRATEFUL FOR...

DATE: _____

_____
_____
_____
_____
_____
_____
_____

SOMETHING AWESOME THAT HAPPENED TODAY

_____
_____
_____
_____
_____
_____
_____
_____
_____

MY LEVEL OF HAPPINESS

TODAY I AM GRATEFUL FOR...

DATE: _____

_____

_____

_____

_____

_____

_____

_____

SOMETHING AWESOME THAT HAPPENED TODAY

_____

_____

_____

_____

_____

_____

_____

_____

_____

MY LEVEL OF HAPPINESS

TODAY I AM GRATEFUL FOR...

DATE: _____

_____
_____
_____
_____
_____
_____
_____

SOMETHING AWESOME THAT HAPPENED TODAY

_____
_____
_____
_____
_____
_____
_____
_____
_____

MY LEVEL OF HAPPINESS

TODAY I AM GRATEFUL FOR...

DATE: _____

_____

_____

_____

_____

_____

_____

SOMETHING AWESOME THAT HAPPENED TODAY

_____

_____

_____

_____

_____

_____

_____

_____

MY LEVEL OF HAPPINESS

TODAY I AM GRATEFUL FOR...

DATE: _____

_____

_____

_____

_____

_____

_____

_____

SOMETHING AWESOME THAT HAPPENED TODAY

_____

_____

_____

_____

_____

_____

_____

_____

_____

_____

MY LEVEL OF HAPPINESS

TODAY I AM GRATEFUL FOR...   DATE: _____

_____

_____

_____

_____

_____

_____

_____

SOMETHING AWESOME THAT HAPPENED TODAY

MY LEVEL OF HAPPINESS

_____

_____

_____

_____

_____

_____

_____

_____

TODAY I AM GRATEFUL FOR...

DATE: _____

_____
_____
_____
_____
_____
_____
_____
_____
_____

SOMETHING AWESOME THAT HAPPENED TODAY

_____
_____
_____
_____
_____
_____
_____
_____
_____

MY LEVEL OF HAPPINESS

TODAY I AM GRATEFUL FOR...

DATE: _____

_____

_____

_____

_____

_____

_____

_____

SOMETHING AWESOME THAT HAPPENED TODAY

_____

_____

_____

_____

_____

_____

_____

_____

_____

_____

MY LEVEL OF HAPPINESS

TODAY I AM GRATEFUL FOR...

DATE: _____

_____

_____

_____

_____

_____

_____

_____

SOMETHING AWESOME THAT HAPPENED TODAY

_____

_____

_____

_____

_____

_____

_____

_____

_____

MY LEVEL OF HAPPINESS

TODAY I AM GRATEFUL FOR...

DATE: _____

_____
_____
_____
_____
_____
_____
_____

SOMETHING AWESOME THAT HAPPENED TODAY

_____
_____
_____
_____
_____
_____
_____
_____
_____

MY LEVEL OF HAPPINESS

TODAY I AM GRATEFUL FOR...

DATE: _____

_____

_____

_____

_____

_____

_____

_____

SOMETHING AWESOME THAT HAPPENED TODAY

_____

_____

_____

_____

_____

_____

_____

_____

MY LEVEL OF HAPPINESS

TODAY I AM GRATEFUL FOR...

DATE: _____

_____

_____

_____

_____

_____

_____

_____

SOMETHING AWESOME THAT HAPPENED TODAY

_____

_____

_____

_____

_____

_____

_____

_____

MY LEVEL OF HAPPINESS

TODAY I AM GRATEFUL FOR...

DATE: _____

_____

_____

_____

_____

_____

_____

_____

_____

SOMETHING AWESOME THAT HAPPENED TODAY

_____

_____

_____

_____

_____

_____

_____

_____

_____

MY LEVEL OF HAPPINESS

TODAY I AM GRATEFUL FOR...

DATE: _____

_____

_____

_____

_____

_____

_____

_____

_____

SOMETHING AWESOME THAT HAPPENED TODAY

_____

_____

_____

_____

_____

_____

_____

_____

MY LEVEL OF HAPPINESS

TODAY I AM GRATEFUL FOR...

DATE: _____

_____
_____
_____
_____
_____
_____
_____

SOMETHING AWESOME THAT HAPPENED TODAY

_____
_____
_____
_____
_____
_____
_____
_____
_____
_____

MY LEVEL OF HAPPINESS

TODAY I AM GRATEFUL FOR...

DATE: _____

_____

_____

_____

_____

_____

_____

_____

_____

SOMETHING AWESOME THAT HAPPENED TODAY

_____

_____

_____

_____

_____

_____

_____

_____

_____

MY LEVEL OF HAPPINESS

TODAY I AM GRATEFUL FOR...

DATE: _____

_____

_____

_____

_____

_____

_____

_____

SOMETHING AWESOME THAT HAPPENED TODAY

_____

_____

_____

_____

_____

_____

_____

_____

_____

_____

MY LEVEL OF HAPPINESS

TODAY I AM GRATEFUL FOR...

DATE: _____

_____

_____

_____

_____

_____

_____

_____

SOMETHING AWESOME THAT HAPPENED TODAY

_____

_____

_____

_____

_____

_____

_____

_____

_____

MY LEVEL OF HAPPINESS

TODAY I AM GRATEFUL FOR...

DATE: _____

SOMETHING AWESOME THAT HAPPENED TODAY

MY LEVEL OF HAPPINESS

TODAY I AM GRATEFUL FOR...

DATE: _____

_____

_____

_____

_____

_____

_____

_____

SOMETHING AWESOME THAT HAPPENED TODAY

_____

_____

_____

_____

_____

_____

_____

_____

MY LEVEL OF HAPPINESS

TODAY I AM GRATEFUL FOR...

DATE: _____

_____

_____

_____

_____

_____

_____

_____

_____

SOMETHING AWESOME THAT HAPPENED TODAY

_____

_____

_____

_____

_____

_____

_____

_____

_____

_____

MY LEVEL OF HAPPINESS

TODAY I AM GRATEFUL FOR...

DATE: _____

_____

_____

_____

_____

_____

_____

_____

SOMETHING AWESOME THAT HAPPENED TODAY

_____

_____

_____

_____

_____

_____

_____

_____

_____

MY LEVEL OF HAPPINESS

TODAY I AM GRATEFUL FOR...   DATE: _____

_____
_____
_____
_____
_____
_____
_____

SOMETHING AWESOME THAT HAPPENED TODAY

_____
_____
_____
_____
_____
_____
_____
_____

MY LEVEL OF HAPPINESS

TODAY I AM GRATEFUL FOR...   DATE: _____

_____

_____

_____

_____

_____

_____

_____

SOMETHING AWESOME THAT HAPPENED TODAY

_____

_____

_____

_____

_____

_____

_____

_____

MY LEVEL OF HAPPINESS

TODAY I AM GRATEFUL FOR...   DATE: _____

_____

_____

_____

_____

_____

_____

_____

_____

SOMETHING AWESOME THAT HAPPENED TODAY

_____

_____

_____

_____

_____

_____

_____

_____

_____

_____

MY LEVEL OF HAPPINESS

TODAY I AM GRATEFUL FOR...

DATE: _____

_____
_____
_____
_____
_____
_____
_____
_____

SOMETHING AWESOME THAT HAPPENED TODAY

_____
_____
_____
_____
_____
_____
_____
_____
_____

MY LEVEL OF HAPPINESS

TODAY I AM GRATEFUL FOR...

DATE: _____

_____
_____
_____
_____
_____
_____
_____
_____

SOMETHING AWESOME THAT HAPPENED TODAY

_____
_____
_____
_____
_____
_____
_____
_____
_____
_____

MY LEVEL OF HAPPINESS

TODAY I AM GRATEFUL FOR...

DATE: _____

_____
_____
_____
_____
_____
_____
_____

SOMETHING AWESOME THAT HAPPENED TODAY

_____
_____
_____
_____
_____
_____
_____
_____
_____
_____

MY LEVEL OF HAPPINESS

TODAY I AM GRATEFUL FOR...

DATE: _____

_____

_____

_____

_____

_____

_____

SOMETHING AWESOME THAT HAPPENED TODAY

_____

_____

_____

_____

_____

_____

_____

_____

MY LEVEL OF HAPPINESS

TODAY I AM GRATEFUL FOR...

DATE: _____

_____

_____

_____

_____

_____

_____

_____

SOMETHING AWESOME THAT HAPPENED TODAY

_____

_____

_____

_____

_____

_____

_____

_____

_____

_____

MY LEVEL OF HAPPINESS

TODAY I AM GRATEFUL FOR...   DATE: _____

_____
_____
_____
_____
_____
_____
_____

SOMETHING AWESOME THAT HAPPENED TODAY

_____
_____
_____
_____
_____
_____
_____
_____
_____
_____
_____

MY LEVEL OF HAPPINESS

TODAY I AM GRATEFUL FOR...

DATE:

_____

_____

_____

_____

_____

_____

_____

_____

_____

SOMETHING AWESOME THAT HAPPENED TODAY

_____

_____

_____

_____

_____

_____

_____

_____

_____

_____

_____

MY LEVEL OF HAPPINESS

TODAY I AM GRATEFUL FOR...

DATE: _____

_____
_____
_____
_____
_____
_____
_____

SOMETHING AWESOME THAT HAPPENED TODAY

_____
_____
_____
_____
_____
_____
_____
_____
_____
_____

MY LEVEL OF HAPPINESS

TODAY I AM GRATEFUL FOR...

DATE: _____

_____
_____
_____
_____
_____
_____
_____

SOMETHING AWESOME THAT HAPPENED TODAY

_____
_____
_____
_____
_____
_____
_____
_____
_____
_____

MY LEVEL OF HAPPINESS

TODAY I AM GRATEFUL FOR...

DATE: _____

_____

_____

_____

_____

_____

_____

_____

SOMETHING AWESOME THAT HAPPENED TODAY

_____

_____

_____

_____

_____

_____

_____

_____

_____

MY LEVEL OF HAPPINESS

TODAY I AM GRATEFUL FOR...

DATE: _____

_____
_____
_____
_____
_____
_____
_____
_____
_____

SOMETHING AWESOME THAT HAPPENED TODAY

_____
_____
_____
_____
_____
_____
_____
_____
_____
_____
_____

MY LEVEL OF HAPPINESS

TODAY I AM GRATEFUL FOR...

DATE: _____

_____
_____
_____
_____
_____
_____
_____

SOMETHING AWESOME THAT HAPPENED TODAY

_____
_____
_____
_____
_____
_____
_____
_____
_____
_____
_____

MY LEVEL OF HAPPINESS

TODAY I AM GRATEFUL FOR...

DATE: _____

_____

_____

_____

_____

_____

_____

_____

SOMETHING AWESOME THAT HAPPENED TODAY

_____

_____

_____

_____

_____

_____

_____

_____

_____

_____

MY LEVEL OF HAPPINESS

TODAY I AM GRATEFUL FOR...

DATE: _____

_____

_____

_____

_____

_____

_____

_____

SOMETHING AWESOME THAT HAPPENED TODAY

_____

_____

_____

_____

_____

_____

_____

_____

_____

_____

MY LEVEL OF HAPPINESS

TODAY I AM GRATEFUL FOR...

DATE: _____

_____

_____

_____

_____

_____

_____

_____

_____

_____

SOMETHING AWESOME THAT HAPPENED TODAY

_____

_____

_____

_____

_____

_____

_____

_____

_____

_____

MY LEVEL OF HAPPINESS

TODAY I AM GRATEFUL FOR...

DATE: _____

_____

_____

_____

_____

_____

_____

_____

SOMETHING AWESOME THAT HAPPENED TODAY

_____

_____

_____

_____

_____

_____

_____

_____

_____

_____

MY LEVEL OF HAPPINESS

TODAY I AM GRATEFUL FOR...

DATE: _____

_____
_____
_____
_____
_____
_____
_____
_____

SOMETHING AWESOME THAT HAPPENED TODAY

_____
_____
_____
_____
_____
_____
_____
_____
_____
_____
_____

MY LEVEL OF HAPPINESS

TODAY I AM GRATEFUL FOR...

DATE: _____

_____

_____

_____

_____

_____

_____

_____

SOMETHING AWESOME THAT HAPPENED TODAY

_____

_____

_____

_____

_____

_____

_____

_____

_____

MY LEVEL OF HAPPINESS

TODAY I AM GRATEFUL FOR...

DATE: _____

_____
_____
_____
_____
_____
_____
_____
_____

SOMETHING AWESOME THAT HAPPENED TODAY

_____
_____
_____
_____
_____
_____
_____
_____
_____
_____
_____

MY LEVEL OF HAPPINESS

TODAY I AM GRATEFUL FOR...

DATE: ....

_____

_____

_____

_____

_____

_____

_____

SOMETHING AWESOME THAT HAPPENED TODAY

_____

_____

_____

_____

_____

_____

_____

_____

_____

_____

MY LEVEL OF HAPPINESS

TODAY I AM GRATEFUL FOR...

DATE: _____

_____
_____
_____
_____
_____
_____
_____
_____

SOMETHING AWESOME THAT HAPPENED TODAY

_____
_____
_____
_____
_____
_____
_____
_____
_____
_____

MY LEVEL OF HAPPINESS

TODAY I AM GRATEFUL FOR...

DATE: _____

_____

_____

_____

_____

_____

_____

_____

SOMETHING AWESOME THAT HAPPENED TODAY

_____

_____

_____

_____

_____

_____

_____

_____

MY LEVEL OF HAPPINESS

TODAY I AM GRATEFUL FOR...   DATE: _____

_____

_____

_____

_____

_____

_____

_____

SOMETHING AWESOME THAT HAPPENED TODAY

_____

_____

_____

_____

_____

_____

_____

_____

_____

MY LEVEL OF HAPPINESS

TODAY I AM GRATEFUL FOR...

DATE:

_____

_____

_____

_____

_____

_____

_____

SOMETHING AWESOME THAT HAPPENED TODAY

_____

_____

_____

_____

_____

_____

_____

_____

_____

MY LEVEL OF HAPPINESS

TODAY I AM GRATEFUL FOR...

DATE: _____

_____

_____

_____

_____

_____

_____

_____

SOMETHING AWESOME THAT HAPPENED TODAY

_____

_____

_____

_____

_____

_____

_____

_____

_____

MY LEVEL OF HAPPINESS

TODAY I AM GRATEFUL FOR...

DATE: _____

_____

_____

_____

_____

_____

_____

_____

SOMETHING AWESOME THAT HAPPENED TODAY

_____

_____

_____

_____

_____

_____

_____

_____

_____

_____

_____

MY LEVEL OF HAPPINESS

TODAY I AM GRATEFUL FOR...

DATE: _____

_____
_____
_____
_____
_____
_____
_____
_____

SOMETHING AWESOME THAT HAPPENED TODAY

_____
_____
_____
_____
_____
_____
_____
_____
_____
_____

MY LEVEL OF HAPPINESS

TODAY I AM GRATEFUL FOR...

DATE:

SOMETHING AWESOME THAT HAPPENED TODAY

MY LEVEL OF HAPPINESS

TODAY I AM GRATEFUL FOR...

DATE:

SOMETHING AWESOME THAT HAPPENED TODAY

MY LEVEL OF HAPPINESS

TODAY I AM GRATEFUL FOR...

DATE:

_____
_____
_____
_____
_____
_____
_____

SOMETHING AWESOME THAT HAPPENED TODAY

_____
_____
_____
_____
_____
_____
_____
_____
_____
_____

MY LEVEL OF HAPPINESS

TODAY I AM GRATEFUL FOR...

DATE: _____

_____
_____
_____
_____
_____
_____
_____
_____
_____

SOMETHING AWESOME THAT HAPPENED TODAY

_____
_____
_____
_____
_____
_____
_____
_____
_____
_____
_____

MY LEVEL OF HAPPINESS

TODAY I AM GRATEFUL FOR...

DATE: _____

_____

_____

_____

_____

_____

_____

_____

SOMETHING AWESOME THAT HAPPENED TODAY

_____

_____

_____

_____

_____

_____

_____

_____

_____

_____

MY LEVEL OF HAPPINESS

TODAY I AM GRATEFUL FOR...

DATE: _____

_____

_____

_____

_____

_____

_____

_____

_____

SOMETHING AWESOME THAT HAPPENED TODAY

_____

_____

_____

_____

_____

_____

_____

_____

_____

_____

_____

MY LEVEL OF HAPPINESS

TODAY I AM GRATEFUL FOR...

DATE: _____

_____

_____

_____

_____

_____

_____

_____

SOMETHING AWESOME THAT HAPPENED TODAY

_____

_____

_____

_____

_____

_____

_____

_____

_____

MY LEVEL OF HAPPINESS

TODAY I AM GRATEFUL FOR...   DATE: _____

_____

_____

_____

_____

_____

_____

_____

SOMETHING AWESOME THAT HAPPENED TODAY

_____

_____

_____

_____

_____

_____

_____

_____

_____

MY LEVEL OF HAPPINESS

TODAY I AM GRATEFUL FOR...

DATE: _____

_____

_____

_____

_____

_____

_____

_____

SOMETHING AWESOME THAT HAPPENED TODAY

_____

_____

_____

_____

_____

_____

_____

_____

_____

_____

MY LEVEL OF HAPPINESS

TODAY I AM GRATEFUL FOR...

DATE: _____

_____
_____
_____
_____
_____
_____
_____
_____

SOMETHING AWESOME THAT HAPPENED TODAY

MY LEVEL OF HAPPINESS

TODAY I AM GRATEFUL FOR...

DATE: _____

_____
_____
_____
_____
_____
_____
_____

SOMETHING AWESOME THAT HAPPENED TODAY

_____
_____
_____
_____
_____
_____
_____
_____
_____
_____

MY LEVEL OF HAPPINESS

TODAY I AM GRATEFUL FOR...

DATE: _____

_____
_____
_____
_____
_____
_____
_____
_____
_____

SOMETHING AWESOME THAT HAPPENED TODAY

_____
_____
_____
_____
_____
_____
_____
_____
_____
_____

MY LEVEL OF HAPPINESS

TODAY I AM GRATEFUL FOR...

DATE: _____

_____

_____

_____

_____

_____

_____

_____

SOMETHING AWESOME THAT HAPPENED TODAY

_____

_____

_____

_____

_____

_____

_____

_____

_____

MY LEVEL OF HAPPINESS

TODAY I AM GRATEFUL FOR...

DATE: _____

_____
_____
_____
_____
_____
_____
_____
_____

SOMETHING AWESOME THAT HAPPENED TODAY

_____
_____
_____
_____
_____
_____
_____
_____
_____
_____
_____

MY LEVEL OF HAPPINESS

TODAY I AM GRATEFUL FOR...

DATE: _____

_____
_____
_____
_____
_____
_____
_____
_____
_____

SOMETHING AWESOME THAT HAPPENED TODAY

_____
_____
_____
_____
_____
_____
_____
_____
_____
_____
_____

MY LEVEL OF HAPPINESS

TODAY I AM GRATEFUL FOR...

DATE: _____

_____

_____

_____

_____

_____

_____

_____

SOMETHING AWESOME THAT HAPPENED TODAY

_____

_____

_____

_____

_____

_____

_____

_____

_____

MY LEVEL OF HAPPINESS

TODAY I AM GRATEFUL FOR...

DATE: _____

_____
_____
_____
_____
_____
_____
_____

SOMETHING AWESOME THAT HAPPENED TODAY

_____
_____
_____
_____
_____
_____
_____
_____
_____

MY LEVEL OF HAPPINESS

TODAY I AM GRATEFUL FOR...   DATE: _____

_____

_____

_____

_____

_____

_____

_____

_____

SOMETHING AWESOME THAT HAPPENED TODAY

MY LEVEL OF HAPPINESS

Made in the USA
Middletown, DE
05 September 2020

18472621R00053